The Emma Press Anthology of
FATHERHOOD

Other Emma Press anthologies:

The Emma Press Anthology of Mildly Erotic Verse
A Poetic Primer for Love and Seduction: Naso was my Tutor
The Emma Press Anthology of Motherhood
The Emma Press Anthology of Homesickness and Exile (Sept 2014)
Best Friends Forever (Dec 2014)

The Emma Press Picks:

The Flower and the Plough, by Rachel Piercey
The Emmores, by Richard O'Brien
The Held and the Lost, by Kristen Roberts
Captain Love and the Five Joaquins, by John Clegg

Pamphlets:

Raspberries for the Ferry, by Andrew Wynn Owen
Ikhda, by Ikhda, by Ikhda Ayuning Maharsi
The Dead Snail Diaries, by Jamie McGarry (Jul 2014)
Myrtle, by Ruth Wiggins (Nov 2014)
If I Lay on my Back I Saw Nothing but Naked Women,
  by Jacqueline Saphra (Nov 2014)

The Emma Press Anthology of

FATHERHOOD

EDITED BY RACHEL PIERCEY AND EMMA WRIGHT

with poems from Alan Buckley, John Canfield,
Oliver Comins, Nathan Curnow, Hugh Dunkerley,
Flora de Falbe, Sarah Fletcher, John Fuller, Jeremy
Grant, John Grey, Robert Hamberger, James Harris,
Sara Hirsch, Lynn Hoffman, Kirsten Irving, Max Maher,
Martin Malone, Harry Man, Katrina Naomi, Richard
O'Brien, Rachel Piercey, Stevie Ronnie, Jacqueline
Saphra, John Saunders, Tom Sheehan, Di Slaney, Jon
Stone, Richard Thompson and Jerrold Yam

THE EMMA PRESS

THE EMMA PRESS

First published in Great Britain in 2014
by The Emma Press Ltd

Poems copyright © individual copyright holders 2014
Selection copyright © Rachel Piercey and Emma Wright 2014
Illustrations and introduction copyright © Emma Wright 2014

ISBN 978-1-910139-00-4

A CIP catalogue record of this book
is available from the British Library.

Printed and bound in Great Britain
by Letterworks, Reading.

theemmapress.com
editor@theemmapress.com

Contents

Introduction

For a book full of confessions and confrontations, *The Emma Press Anthology of Fatherhood* contains remarkably little direct communication. Poets commune with lost fathers in addresses destined never to reach their subject, and explain themselves to children who are too young to understand. Poems such as Oliver Comins' 'Brown Leather Gloves' and Sara Hirsch's 'Tonight Matthew' find resolution and peace beyond the grave, while Di Slaney's 'On the forestry commission track' and Rich Thompson's 'And he the maul' analyse old memories for clues and redemption. In their many ways – and often through some sense of distance – all the poets convey great depth of feeling, and offer a fascinating insight into the state of fatherhood in the twenty-first century.

When Rachel Piercey, my co-editor, and I were planning the call for submissions to this book, we expected some responses to focus on the pressures of modern fatherhood. The role of the father has expanded rapidly over the last few decades and I thought this would be reflected in poems about the pressure of living up to society's expectations of what a father should now be. Instead, poets seemed more preoccupied with their own fathers and the impact their approach to parenting had on the poets' lives. Jerrold Yam's 'Ornament' and John Saunders' 'My father is the breeze that opens the shed door' explore the impassive twentieth-century father who appears throughout the book, reflecting the enduring legacy of the traditional father figure.

The other main subject of submissions was new parenthood and, in the book, poems such as Jeremy Grant's 'Rubáiyát' and Hugh Dunkerley's 'Coming Home' document the vulnerability of new fathers in heart-breaking detail. Their emotional openness sits in direct opposition to the buttoned-down fathers elsewhere in the book, and the starkness of this contrast opens up a moving dialogue between fathers of the past and fathers of the present.

The strong and silent father is retired with tremendous poignancy but – strikingly – little regret: the modern fathers are ready to experience everything their new role holds, and while individual fathers are mourned, the traditions restraining twentieth-century fathers are not. As Nathan Curnow's 'Bath-Towel Wings' and Kirsten Irving's 'Mysterious Work' explore, the real pressure of modern fatherhood is not so much the weight of new responsibilities, unrequired of their fathers, but more about living up to men's expectations of themselves; to be the best that they can.

The book has become a snapshot of our times, capturing this period when the sons of twentieth-century fathers are becoming fathers themselves. But the scope of *The Emma Press Anthology of Fatherhood* is much wider than this, and the poems also form a compelling study of the fundamental father-child relationship, the battlefield and haven which has been redefined with every birth for millennia. Poems such as Richard O'Brien's 'Queen Dick' and Jon Stone's 'Tiberius and the Kid' remind us that parenthood has never been easy, while Lynn Hoffman ('my hero') and Tom Sheehan ('Father) attest to the possibility of mutual understanding in any era; and Alan Buckley's 'Joinery Work' shows that reconciliation can occur at any time. This is a book where the best of intentions shine through repeatedly and sons try not to repeat their fathers' mistakes, while maintaining the legacy of their love. The past can be frustrating and saddening, as well as profoundly moving, but the book looks to the future and finds modern fathers trying their hardest with care, awe and love.

Emma Wright
WINNERSH
May 2014

The Emma Press Anthology of Fatherhood

Bath–Towel Wings

Embracing herself in bath-towel wings,
corners clutched with tight, pink fists,
she waits for pyjamas in the centre of the room,
warmly dripping what is left of the bath.
I don't want to die, she says, and if I could waive
death somehow, waive it like a day of school –
If I could write her a note or simply wrestle it,
the way I contort her into armholes –
I tell her that I love her but she's heard it before.
She wants to know where we go after this.
She believes in Santa. I can't let her trust Jesus.
Yes, your heart stops working and your lungs.
I want to tell her that life gets busier
which means there is less time to worry.
If there is a trick it's not to grieve too much.
The mystery must be lived, hope is important
and fear – I get the two mixed up. But the end is coming
without permission, whether I spell it exactly or not
and these wings, this warmth, whatever we enact,
will never come to pass without love.

Brown Leather Gloves

These are my Father's gloves
with which I am wrestling
as I walk down to the station
on another crisp morning
of frosted cars in a frozen suburb.

Who's holding whose hands now?
Inside the fingers there's
more of him than there is of me –
all those years of rubbed skin and sweat.

Leather gives a better grip,
doesn't really overcome the cold.
But it's better than nothing,
this thin layer of brown
which keeps the weather off.

On the platform
I remove one Father,
reach out to greet a friend.
My other Father holds me steady.

Tiberius and the Kid

Who sprawls across their island-throne,
dinosaurish, eek of bone,
taciturn, stubborn and terribly stern,
terrible, blunt and serious?
        Old emperor Tiberius.

And who's his imp, whose temples burn
with an eagerness to learn,
impious, impertinent, impatient, vain,
none cleverer, none stupider?
        The usurper, Kid Jupiter.

Who rises early, dons their gown,
plucks the blood-sun from its dawn,
chunks it up with a grapefruit knife,
hands out half and asks, 'Enough?'
bitterly, burdenedly, terminally gruff,
buffeted, tethered, tenderly rough,
terse, tight-lipped, imperious?
        The weathered bulk of Tiberius.

Who takes that meal and wolfs it down,
asks for more with a blazing grin,
licks the plate that is his life
and moves to howl, then sing, then laugh,
jumped-up jake from boot to cuff,
lucid, inscrutable, brutish but beautiful,
jubilant, jagged, wicked, immutable,
juice-flecked?
        The indubita-
bly super-charged Kid Jupiter.

And who looks on him, spent, delirious,
dim star to his Sirius,
too tired to be furious?
The one who made him: Tiberius.

Digitalis

Between his first and third heart attack
passed my father's Summer of Love.
An unknown younger man came back:

my ear-ring was no longer mocked
– nor the tattoo of an arrowed dove –
between his first and third heart attack.

A sudden awareness of hip-hop and rap,
a shuffling of beat groups with dub,
as an unknown younger man came back.

I'd come across him trying on hats
and found him once weeping at foxgloves
between his first and third heart attack.

Aware that given time is not given back,
he started bending lifelong rules enough
to let me see the younger man come back.

Dad was Dylan, McCartney, Jack Kerouac
in that last fond Summer of Love
between his first and third heart attack
when an unknown younger man came back.

Shift

I have seen the men in fluorescent orange
more times this week than is, strictly speaking, wise,
as they gather around the station entrance
preparing to walk the closed-down lines;
when I catch the eyes of one, they seem to say
'You do know it's a weeknight, son?'

As it happens, I do and I weave my way
down a neon-lit road as the many headed
Hi-Vis Hydra prepares to descend, like Orpheus
or Persephone or some other appropriate
clever-dick reference, to the unique black below.

This scene ignites a vapour trail of thoughts:
my solemn father sinking down into a mine
for another night, trading away a lunar sky
for artificial daylight, returning at dawn
to the synthesised gloaming of bedroom curtains
drawn through summer days.

Or it *would*, but for the fact I'm drunk
on a weeknight again, odysseying home
from a sedentary day in a diode-lit room
and when, through the darkness, I get to my bed
I'll be out, as it were, like a light.

My Parents' Poem

won't be set in couplets,
                          certainly won't rhyme.
I'll let you guess the refrain,
                          his envoi,
after a volley of verbs.
                          It will be Hughesian, Plathian,
well, from that era. It will be brief,
                          yet I won't understand it all.
A work of juvenilia,
                          their poem will try to marry certain ideals.
It will be written in the past tense
                          by another woman.

Wave Machine

Sirens and lights introduce it, hook us in.
We're a wet crowd paying dry money to be rocked
today by artificial tides. Your brothers begin
a slow sway down the deep end, while we're knocked
and doused in the shallows. You scoop water
in armfuls over you, sluice your skin with a belly-dive
wild as instinct. Jump the waves, my wringing daughter.
When one floods your mouth I pat your back. I must drive
you home tomorrow: your place, not mine.
You'll make me count how many days until
you see me, using my fingers and yours to reach thirteen.
Dance for every minute that matters: when we roll
or bump together now, rinsed as pebbles over
and over, and you sing in my ear.

Coming Home

You should still be in the womb –
a tender fish hooked too early –
as I carry you outside for the first time,
a cold westerly whipping around
the hospital's concrete canyons,
wrinkling your features.

In the waiting car we struggle
with the oversized child seat
and you begin to wail,
a tremulous, high-pitched call of distress,
your tiny limbs jerking with unaccustomed freedom.

I drive through rush-hour traffic
as if the slightest bump could shatter you,
your mother's head pressed close to yours
in the rearview mirror.

At home we will you to sleep,
pace up and down with your curled frame
clamped to our chests,
but nothing will comfort you,
nothing make up for the loss
of your first home in this world:

the ward with its fluorescent hum,
its constantly chattering monitors,
the small plastic tub where you lay swaddled
for three weeks in a womb of white
antiseptic-smelling blankets.

Four Years from Now, Walking with My Daughter

How easily she fits into my country skin
between the crag and the forest where we begin
to dawdle. It's late now for paradise (that hidden
place where the burn has cut its path) and given
how years may pass, perhaps I'll keep it as my own.
We stop and sit with nothing but the grass she combs.
                        I'm nervous for the time that will
come; of trains, platforms, waving. Here it's still
in the midst of lambing. We listen to a tractor –
count a flock of crows like seconds. Laughter.
One lamb finds the only tear in the fence there is.
She bleats and makes for a clearing in the trees.

Tonight Matthew

i.m. Clifford Green

I'm rushing so fast through life
it's like I'm on a high-speed rail
like I'm a dog going round and round in circles
but never quite catching up with its tail
and as I sail through time aboard this super power
hundred mile an hour train
watching the days fade into a blur
through the wind-whipped window pane
I wonder how I will ever get off again.

See, I missed my stop.

I missed my stop in 2001
and for twelve years I've been on the run
trying to get back to where the journey began.

I don't know if you remember that November?
It was the mess of you losing your hair
and the stress of hospital appointments
and mumbled greetings on the stair
with me never quite sure if you were really there with me
or somewhere in your memory.
It was nervous nights in front of the TV
with you laughing at Stars In Their Eyes
even though it wasn't even funny –
or at least it wasn't meant to be
and you repeating
Tonight Matthew I'm going to be
over and over again until

Mum reminded you to take your pill.
Tonight Matthew I'm going to be
like a broken record –
and for the first time I realised that you really were ill.

You tried to explain cancer to me.
See, there's something wrong with my head you said
That's why I'm always in bed you said
That's what the pills are for
but instead I just saw the hallway side
of your bedroom door
and mum going to Parents' Evening alone
and you couldn't drive me to school anymore
and suddenly you weren't at home
but a cracking voice on the end of the phone
and to twelve year old me –
that's not what dads were supposed to be.

So I boarded my train
and for twelve years I've been running from the words
The cancer has spread to my brain
pretending like the time never came
where I stood at a grave that bore my father's name.

And it's been a good ride.
I never shied away from anything –
and I've tried to not be stubborn like you,
but I've always kept my pride
and I even found someone prepared to travel at my side –
and I told him all about you.

But now
after twelve years on the track

each summer spent
each promise meant
at each point on the map
each memory I've made collected like postcards
lining the bottom of my rucksack –
after twelve years of travels
I think it might be time to go back.

Because soon
I will have not known you
for more time than I knew you –
and I can't get over that.

So I'm standing before you tonight
fresh from the station, after nearly a whole generation
and although I stand before you as Sara Hirsch
(a name distinctly different
from the one you gave me at my birth)
with a world of experience
from twelve more years on this earth
Tonight Matthew I'm going to be Sara Green.
Tonight Matthew I'm going to tell my Dad
all the things I've done and seen
and he's going to be the father
that for twelve years he hasn't been.
Tonight Matthew I'm going to remember
because on the 25th of November
I will reach the halfway mark –
and every day after that will take me further from the start
like the earth moving round the sun too quickly
so it's always getting dark
and as the earth spins it will take us
further and further apart.

Tonight Matthew I'm going to know him like this
for the very last time
I'm going to take this moment
to commit his memory to mine –

and then tomorrow

I will be wearing his green woollen jumper
and I will put the photo of him I have
from before it all went wrong
into the pocket of my rucksack
and my headphones will blare out his favourite song
and I will catch the first train that comes along
and I won't look back.

Daughter

Once inside my head
The thought is hard to get out:
    Another daughter.

You were never ours.
Photographs showed you missing
    And no one noticed.

Intention was blind:
How near was your conception
    We shall never know.

The disqualified
Candidates can't believe the
    Office is unfilled.

You don't exist, but
Nobody can take your place:
    That space has been booked.

Three faces suggest
The fourth: compass points of the
    Parental axes.

Words like little loves
Presiding over a map
    For future journeys.

Prospero's secret
Sadness: I had peopled else
    This isle with daughters.

Only the subject
Of unuseful poetry:
What never occurred.

After 'Loss of Sons'

from Egils saga Skallagrímssonar,
possibly by Snorri Sturluson

Translate this word as *wagon man*;
wagon man must mean Thor.
Snorri means that Egill
has no praise
for this god any more.

The scribe understands
that the scribe before him understood
what Snorri says
Egill felt.

Egill found his son drowned
on the beach.
Egill found his son's joints
long seized up

like his own tongue
when he swung the coffin on his shoulders
and stumbled it from home.

Now Egill trusts in Odin
for a new song.
Egill trusts in Odin
for the words
to loosen up his son's limbs
so he walks by Egill's shoulder
through the never-ending future
of the verse.

And soon Egill – the boy who split
his schoolmate's skull,
the raider and the warrior –
unbolts his door
and allows himself to eat again.
He lives to be an old man.

A thousand years on,
neither of them are missed.

But the reader's stomach
still twists
when Egill discovers that his son,
the only son left to love,
can no longer be spoken with,
only spoken of.

Meeting My Fathers

Derek, first to arrive, is in Barbour shirt, sensible trousers;
Sonnie wears denims, shirt open to mid-chest,
his silver St Christopher hanging, heavy.
I don't know why I'm here. Derek has left
his collection of international friends in the saloon bar.
Sonnie unwraps his Toby jugs, sets them in a circle,
like an invocation –
then I remember, he's already dead.
My mother works behind the bar.
I pay for the drinks.
She looks at both men, can't decide between them,
can't imagine what she ever saw in either.
My sister wipes our table.
It's been so long, Derek doesn't recognise her,
wanders back to his friends.
Sonnie starts to disintegrate, becomes a slick,
something my mother will have to clear up.
I can probably sell the medallion.

Ornament

My father has few things to protect.
In our house where laughter flirts
effortlessly with a history
of loneliness, sometimes
edifying each other, as two people
stranded on an island may behave,
the magnificent koi pond is
his honour and glory. Cut in black marble,
water unloosed over the imposing
shoulders of an obsidian wall, it seems,
as I grow older, to be more perfect
for my father's affections
than I can ever be, how virtuous
its talent for turning the commonplace
beautiful. On nights when
my father is somewhere else
I stoop over its edge, cautious as
deer approaching the open, water
so still it could be land, my body
ready to navigate a world he has
carved out of absence and longing,
where we are together again.

Handshake

When I speak
to my father now,
he is always
wearing the same
clothes – olive green
cap, matching
zip-up jacket,
brown corduroys
slightly too short.

His eyes are still
crow-sharp
behind thick,
black-framed
glasses, but death
has loosened him,
suppled his throat,
so nothing now
is left unspoken.

I move to embrace
him; catch myself.
My right hand
drops, meets his
in a firm grasp.
My left hand
hovers in mid-air,
not knowing where
it should land.

My father is the breeze that opens the shed door

or that's how it felt this morning,
my memory of him
a faded face, his presence
nudged by chance
like the breeze, or his photograph
in ceremonial marching uniform,
green velvet and brocade –
more seventeenth-century cavalier than carpenter.

He taught me most of what I know,
rarely looked to the future,
preferred the livery of the past,
dropped defining history dates,
recited lines of verse.
There was pride in his words,
the lauding of learning –
as though knowledge was authority.

If his ghost appeared to me now
would it be wearing regalia or dungarees?
And the door that blew open –
four by one planed red deal,
tongue and groove,
one and three quarter battens,
three lever mortise lock, recessed.

How did I know that?

my hero

he thought i should would want
the thoughts he thinged and threw
and kicked ahead of him

he gave me water wings in winter
twelve pounds of yarn
on the fourth of july

he braced himself to
brace my self
afraid the kindness
he showed the world
would ruin me.

he spared me
from the soft
deafened up his ears
made sure there was no point to miss.

and so when the bearish teacher
who beat the kids
turned himself on me one day
the next day he skipped work
(early subway, new york times, horn & hardart)

and as he walked me to school i feared for little him.
when later the teacher
pale and scared
lent me every courtesy of the schoolyard

from then on i knew that one of us
would do the best we could and
the other could go on looking
at moons of buried antique planets

just a little braver, a little closer to the sun.

A Hundred Billion

A hundred billion sit back like this
scramble and kick, oblivious
to listeners and onlookers

assisted like this at the waist
sperlunking in the dark for 270 days – give or take –
a hundred billion explore their cave by taste

and by touch and by sound
listening out as echoes bounce
while the cave shrinks around them

provoking a claustrophobic final fit and further
a hundred billion sink and think
of deeper dark

but light below is nature's greatest trick
– or gift – in time
a hundred billion warm to it.

The Words

Once upon a time I am born
and my dad tells me a story.

Its cover-boards are bedrock
and sky, and in between

are his words – sun-making,
form-shaping, helping me

to read self and life
with manageably clear eyes –

and also their own delight.
He conjures single words,

graspable jewels
we pick up over and over;

he throws open troves
of spheres, and lightly offers

each one: family, philosophy,
work, the turning coin

of tragedy and comedy,
art and the truth

and blur of science.
He picks, splices and intertwines,

leaves be, adds silence,
casts questions and answers,

shows how language
shines on the fact of mystery

and – worked or rough –
is compass enough.

He makes me maxims
to sew into my pockets

and gives me words
to find fuel and balm

as I go. He makes the first
stretch of stones

on the unwinding road,
then reconciles my story

to the unknown –
tells me setting forth,

tells me telling,
tells me always able to find him

which is finding home.

On the forestry commission track

Deep in the woods, the serious little girl
Rodin-points her chin, evaluates
her mother who doesn't see, waits
to binocularise a bird, while the whirl

and click of dad's patient lens captures two
in the hand, right there on the track.
I want to whisper in her ear, go back
and say that there will always be too few

moments, words will never paint another
picture like this. I want to tell
her to inhale the silence, smell
the dark scent of pine. Your mother

will never be so close to touch, your dad
so proud in that quiet, clever way he had.

The Lapse

You tread the craggy path of the lapsed choirboy.
You say: 'God is perfect, he is made of perfect:
how *embarrassing*, the scandal – call it "Gardengate" –
what a screw-up, that Eve and Adam sinned.

'God is unblemished as the heavens, if you
tip your head right back and shut your eyes.
Sweetheart,' you say, 'Perfection isn't infinite.
It lives in boxes: a spelling test, or a marriage.

'Just like Pandora's dowry, it lives in boxes,
so let's raise a glass to her, and then to Eve,
for taking that fateful snack
and saving us from ignorance.'

You had this idea which you'd licked over,
like a pebble, till it shone. It was perfect.
It had legs and breasts and was like Jesus –
unavailable.

It should have been my mother, should have
smoothed away my knots and breakages.
I want to call you innocent. My friend says this:
nothing is perfect, only nothing.

Getting There

A Man
City accent – not United! –
condensed
into 5"7.

He filled the expanse
of dusty assemblies
owned by hollow voices
with his deadlift swagger.

Packed into a suit,
his clean-shaven joke
for all of us who knew
the punchline below.

He'd pull up in sunglasses
in the middle of the day
and take us in school buses
out to his gym to train.

He groaned, squatting low
under 100kg loads –
GET UP THERE.
Never surrendered.

Ate whole chickens,
grew wild black beards,
threw his kids about
as they clambered over him,

the stones of his body
in the lawn's sunshine,
while I read nearby
in the shade on the green.

He lifted me
from dark rooms
to moving forward
and making it worth it.

So now when I'm under
a weight that's too heavy,
I remember how I got there,
and I'm climbing all over it.

Lesson for today and tomorrow

Parents, forget good manners,
teach your children how to
right a flipped raft;

a 'thank you' is useless
in a raging river, but a good
foothold, an anchor, tough

taut ropes can tip
that craft and its heavy load
toward the hardiest grip

and float it skyward;
who wants to please an
uncle when the world can

spill, race away; what's a
kiss on the cheek of a maiden
aunt when feet can dig in

against a willful current,
pull hard and clean against
such wrath, such fury

and save an expedition;
no point saying 'please'
to what does as it pleases.

Premature

I

The anaesthetist's still joking with you,
perspiration beading his thick moustache,
when I realise it's already started:

the rummaging in your womb,
your whole slack body shifting on the table,
the heads of the surgeon and his assistant

bobbing in and out of sight
beyond the green wall of cotton
they've rigged up to hide your lower half.

A sharp tug and 'Can you see him?'
you ask, your voice wobbly with panic,
but I can only stand,

legs swimming below me,
as a long needling cry somehow
stitches itself into my brain.

II

What they give me to hold
seems too delicate to be exposed to air,
a small seed shucked early

from the fruit of your womb,
still matted with blood
and waxy with vernix,

a stunned survivor from some terrible accident
slowly coming round,
tiny fists uncurling like ferns.

III

Under his dome, he's swaddled
in oversized baby clothes,
rigged up with an ECG,

apnoea monitor, the machines
chirping and whinnying,
his face below the blue bobble hat

wrinkled like an old man's in sleep.
When we take him out
he cries at the light,

grasps your finger,
watches the semaphore of our smiles
from a far-off place

where words of comfort
can't reach him, where every breath
is a stumbling foothold.

To The Father Walking His Daughter To School

Your daughter is the neon yoyo
of yourself   string arms split-frayed
at blister points   she fits you
    chromosome   to   chromosome
lips thin as eyelid   ventricles
                              contracting
          jumper pink

you speak to her with the
    vocabulary   of a pregnancy
          your smile   matching
her stretchmarked   mother's scars

 your daughter   red socked
                    and four years overdue
    depended on you   postpartum padre
          who swung her like a swing
        loved her vernix to
            vertex   and taught her hopscotch
          on the   medical papers

  you bear her today   on the front gate
        you let her go

Queen Dick

You, iron-fist, you, pugilist,
you cramming my round head with facts,
your disappointment curdling like milk.

I roam the Palace under house arrest,
a prisoner of (you'd say) my idleness.
I pick up trinkets; put them down again.

I feel the Army breathing down my neck,
imagine Christmas:

                              you downstairs,
writing a multi-tome treatise entitled
How to Ruin Everything
for Everyone, while in my room

I wolf down goose by guilty candle-light,
you flesh and blood, the axe laid to the root.

*

In France, signing a false name
to the wife I'll never see again,
without the seal you polished and they smashed,

I hear they've hauled you from the earth,
hoisted you like a rebel flag,
and know my presence was a weakening –

me falling off my horse again,
my warship glugging Channel bilge,
I was the one thing you could not protect.

*

At law against my daughter
for the lands wrecked by my feckless son
whom I (of course) named Oliver,
I feel you in my blood and dream of spikes.

These days I'm lodging with a friend.
I'm eighty-five in Hertfordshire
and hunting nothing but my breath,
the vain spirit trapped in my throat.

In unobtrusive farmer's clothes,
I praise your God of intermittent Love.

Joinery Work

How long did you row with your father,
fighting his brute, inarticulate love –
he couldn't bear it: his eldest daughter
bleeding into womanhood. You left,
picked up your guitar, tin whistle, strode
down the path that led to the rest of the world.
The two of you didn't talk for years, just spoke.
That July we drove south, back to your old
stamping ground. I photographed you – sat
with the sea beyond on a kissing gate;
stood in the wishing chapel up on the hill;
in front of his workshop's roadside wall,
below the sign that carried his name, his trade.
The expression you wore: almost like pride.

Geometry

Remember how, one night not long ago
you told our daughter what you'd read
about infinity? I couldn't understand,
although you drew a diagram
to show that two parallel lines,
if left to run forever, will eventually meet.
Remember when she came home
crying the next day, covered in shame.
In front of everyone her teacher
had dismissed her father's proof.
But I believe you. If you and I had never met
that rainy night in Camden Town,
if that night had never been,
that's where we'd be, each walking the line
towards infinity, searching for the place
where the impossible can happen
and two parallel lines collide.

Mysterious Work

'But, oh wait, even chickens have a spine. That makes you an OCTOPUS!'
– Tommy, *Octodad*

We who cover our beaks with moustaches,
who gobble nonsense at our children, hoping not
to raise their suspicion, that they will not see now
the mess we make of everything, our true form,
we build our dolls from junk, play the game, and, true,
plan our escape. And with every radial flail, a brow
is raised; with every slip, our mantles joggle. Darling,
I would clean the fridge if love would still my muscles,
if hope would give me a churchwork of bones. Be still,
be strong, my branchial heart. My silly rubber crown.
Let me make what I can make from the scraps that are
not yet spilled or stained or scattered. And I will flee
from beneath the sushi knife twisting on its horsehair,
away across country, once more into the sea.

Rubáiyát

for Hal

In the pages of my notebook, each contraction,
and in between, a scribbled calculation:
a Fibonacci sequence in reverse
abandoned near completion – time for action.

*

Your hands are tiny, only one day old.
My finger runs along each fleshy fold.
What doors will they open and how many?
Apart from my hand, whose hands will they hold?

*

The cord is black and shrivelled in a bow.
When you were lifted up, it seemed to glow,
a white, pulsating ribbon, full of blood
that gave you life, until I cut the flow.

*

Liquorice, pesto, mustard, tan: your poo
an ever-changing palette for a new
and vibrant art – Body Expressionism.
My screwed-up face so far your best review.

*

You eat and sleep and when you don't you stare,
as of awareness you become aware.
Your memory will not reach back this far.
These moments disappear into the air.

*

Our morning pram ride from your point of view.
Those white shapes floating in a sea of blue.
This music shaken from the tops of trees.
Through you I learn to see the world anew.

*

I play you David Brubeck's 'Unsquare Dance';
imagine what you'd feel if by chance
you heard it in the future – *déjà vu*
or revelation noted in advance.

*

Your smile is open to interpretation:
happiness or mild constipation?
A winning poker-face we cannot read.
We watch for hours in anticipation.

*

Her body was your cradle long ago,
the only place you thought you'd ever know.
My arms are but a pale imitation.
I try to recreate it even so.

*

First you were nothing, and then you were almost you,
and then you were complete – but still you grew –
a whole and fraction of a future whole,
where one plus one no longer equals two.

Father

His face is made of music,
notes of an order I have yet to know.
The mystics of his hands,
engraved with the timeless,
bear strange anointments.
The salt of his touch, once known,
leaps up past all of pain.
After God and my father
there are no divinities.

And he the maul

We'd start it once the frost was gone.
He'd cut the posts and sharpen them,
I'd peel the bark – slough it off
in white strips dripping sap,
my hands too cold to feel their pull.
And then I'd paint them creosote
while he changed gas and filed the saw
half as big as me.

We'd drive as far as we could go
and then we'd hike the rest –
he with his six posts, I with four,
I with the bar and he the maul.
It was still, damp and gray;
the woods were dark.

Above, the sun, and with it flies –
black clouds that pulsed and
hummed our blood.
We'd never speak – they'd fill
eyes, mouth, and nose;
they'd drown in sweat
then coat the skin.

I'd think to stop, or swat, or spit;
I don't know what he thought.
The maul was sharper than their song.
He'd have a blackened crown of grime
that pressed into his eyes –
the nearest thing I'd see to tears,
my father weeping flies.

Sparks in the Dark

Sparks in the dark: yours, mine
in this vessel swaddled
where lovers collide
once you've got your eye in
there's someone home
tearfrosted window: a bloom, diffuse, barely aglow
but –
(quickbreathing eyeswide bitelip fistclenched)
but there
a swimming nexus, singing forth, forming, growing
out from a singularity
the spark has taken; the dark has broken
definite defiant but vague: glorious paradox

not even our pounding hearts combined keep pace
with this fuzzy little fizzing racing pulse
and our minds combined won't yet fully comprehend
the something from the nothing at the start of it all

Ultrasound

For Loki

The white artery of your spine
hovers beneath a butterfly's ghost;

wings budding into flight
twice a second, heartbeat by heartbeat.

The isthmus of your foot kicks in the fluid –
the pressure of the sensor is ticklish.

With the end of his biro the doctor
circles your magnified hand gloved in light

and this shimmer, this afterthought of air
in the trees is the breath of your mother.

Night-blind you will fumble back
to its anthem through the clicks

of your hardening head.
This song, secret as a light switch,

is how your breathing will be.
The warmth of my wrist on your belly;

your pulse and mine in time –
the first of your strengths is to be loved.

Among the Doctors

'Joseph, Joseph, there in your cattle stall
Joseph, Joseph, what do you make of it all?'
– Jake Thackray, *Joseph*

You always were a dreadful carpenter,
the world in your hands and all thumbs, son.

I soon stopped asking you
to stand across from me
and turn a two-man lathe.

I almost lost a finger
to your thoughts of higher things.

You had your father's eyes,
which is to say not mine,
the day you said you went about his business,
which is to say not mine.

Three days we searched,
tearing up every splinter of the town,
before we saw you
through that gilded grate.

Your mother sent me in,
as if to call you in to dinner
from those learned men.

I'd never seen such green and gold.
I heard it in the words you used.
A kind of sawdust
gumming up my tongue.

You were twelve then.
They doubted you belonged to me.
It was the first time
I had let you go.

This time, we're shaking hands –
your cotton glove, the callused paw
half-shaking in my apron. Go.
Be who you are.

Tell everyone you meet who makes
the finest table legs in Galilee.
Put down your tools. Remember me.

Acknowledgments

'Bath-Towel Wings', by Nathan Curnow, was previously published in *No Other Life But This* (Five Islands Press, 2006).

'Digitalis', by Martin Malone, previously appeared in his debut collection, *The Waiting Hillside* (Templar, 2011), and won the Wivenhoe Poetry Competition in 2011.

'My Parents' Poem', by Katrina Naomi, was published by *The SHOp* in 2012.

'Wave Machine', by Robert Hamberger, was previously published in his collection *The Smug Bridegroom* (Five Leaves Publications, 2002).

'Coming Home', by Hugh Dunkerley, was first published in *The Echo Room*, 2014.

'Fours Years from Now, Walking with My Daughter', by Stevie Ronnie, was first published in the anthology *Gift* (Newcastle Centre for the Literary Arts, 2009) and in his collection *Manifestations* (Red Squirrel Press, 2013).

'Daughter', by John Fuller, was first collected in *The Grey Among the Green* (Chatto and Windus, 1988). Reprinted by permission of The Random House Group Ltd.

'After "Loss of Sons"', by Rachel Piercey, was part of Modern Poets on Viking Poetry, a cultural translation project from the University of Cambridge.

'Meeting My Fathers', by Katrina Naomi, was published in *Smiths Knoll* in 2012.

'Ornament', by Jerrold Yam, was first published in *Antiphon,* Issue 6, 2013.

'Handshake', by Alan Buckley, was previously published in his debut pamphlet *Shiver* (tall-lighthouse, 2009).

'On the forestry commission track', by Di Slaney, has previously been published in *The Interpreter's House*, Issue 50, 2012.

'Getting There', by Max Maher, first appeared in *Notes Magazine*, Issue 13, 2013.

A version of 'Premature', by Hugh Dunkerley, first appeared in *Irish Pages* Vol 6, No 1.

'Geometry', by Jacqueline Saphra, was published in her first full collection, *The Kitchen of Lovely Contraptions* (flipped eye, 2011).

'Father', by Tom Sheehan, was first published in his collection *This Rare Earth & Other Flights* (Little Pot Press, 2003).

'And he the maul', by Richard Thompson, was first published in *Relief Journal*, Issue 3.1, 2009.

'Sparks in the Dark', by James Harris, was first published online by *Amaryllis*.

'Ultrasound', by Harry Man, was first published in *Popshot Magazine* (2012) and has also appeared in *And Other Poems* (2013) and his debut pamphlet, *Lift* (tall-lighthouse, 2013).

About the poets

Alan Buckley's debut pamphlet *Shiver* (tall-lighthouse, 2009) was a Poetry Book Society choice. He has been commended twice in the Bridport Prize, and was short-listed for the inaugural Picador Poetry Prize. He works in Oxford as a psychotherapist, and as a school writer-in-residence for the charity First Story.

John Canfield grew up in Cornwall and now lives in London. His poems have appeared in magazines and anthologies including *Oxford Poetry* XIV.2, *Transom* Issue 5, *Newspaper Taxis* (Seren, 2013), *Coin Opera II* (Sidekick Books, 2013) and *A Poetic Primer for Love and Seduction* (The Emma Press, 2014). He trained as an actor, but due to a clerical error currently works in an accounts department.

Oliver Comins lives and works in West London. He has five children and his early poems were collected in a Mandeville Press pamphlet and *Anvil New Poets Two*. More recently, his poems have appeared in magazines including *The Echo Room*, *The Rialto*, *Warwick Review* and *Yellow Nib*.

Nathan Curnow is the father of four young daughters and is a former editor of *Going Down Swinging*. His work has featured several times in *Best Australian Poems* (Black Inc, 2008, 2010 and 2013) and he has won numerous awards, including the Josephine Ulrick Poetry Prize. His most recent collection, *RADAR*, is available through Walleah Press.

Hugh Dunkerley grew up in Edinburgh and Bath and now lives in Brighton with his wife and young son. He has published one full collection, *Hare* (Cinnamon Press,

2010) and is currently working on a new collection about fatherhood. He was the inaugural West Sussex Poet Laureate from 2000-2012.

Flora de Falbe is in her final year of school in London. She was a Foyle Young Poet in 2011 and 2012 and has read at events including the Ledbury Festival and Chelsea Fringe. Her work is published or forthcoming in *CAKE, Rising, The Emma Press Anthology of Motherhood* and an anthology by Eyewear Publishing.

Sarah Fletcher is a British-American poet. She won a Foyle Young Poet of the Year in 2012 and first and second prize in the Christopher Tower Poetry Prize. Her poems have featured in *The Cadaverine, The London Magazine*, and *The Ofi Press*, and her writing was displayed at Olympic Park during the 2012 Olympics.

John Fuller is an Emeritus Fellow of Magdalen College, Oxford, where for many years he was Tutor in English. Chatto and Windus published his *Collected Poems* in 1996. His latest collection is *Sketches from the Sierra de Tejeda* (Clutag Press, 2013). His prose poem collection *The Dice Cup* is publishing with Chatto in October 2014.

Jeremy Grant lives in Leicestershire with his wife, son, and cat, and teaches at a local sixth form college. His poems have appeared in literary magazines such as *Smiths Knoll, Poetry Nottingham, The French Literary Review* and *The Journal*. He has also co-written teaching guides for the British Film Institute.

John Grey was born in Australia and has been published in *The Lyric, Vallum* and the science fiction anthology *The*

Kennedy Curse. He has work forthcoming in *Bryant Literary Magazine, Natural Bridge, Southern California Review* and *2 Bridges Review.*

Robert Hamberger has been awarded a Hawthornden Fellowship and shortlisted for a Forward prize. He has published six pamphlets. His full-length collections are *Warpaint Angel* (Blackwater Press, 1997), *The Smug Bridegroom* (Five Leaves, 2002) and *Torso* (Redbeck Press, 2007). His fourth collection, *Blue Wallpaper,* is forthcoming with Waterloo Press. He lives in Brighton.

James Harris grew up in Shropshire and is the Collections Officer for the Corinium Museum in Cirencester. At the time of publication, he is brand-new to fatherhood.

Sara Hirsch is based in London and best known for her work as a spoken word artist. She is the current UK Slam Champion and regularly performs at poetry events across the country and abroad. This is Sara's first published poem and she is thrilled to be part of the Anthology.

Lynn Hoffman was born in Brooklyn and lives in Philadelphia. He is the author of *The Short Course in Beer,* leads wine and beer tastings, and enjoys loafing and fishing. His cancer comedy memoir, *Radiation Days*, is publishing in New York in summer 2014.

Kirsten Irving is half of the team behind collaborative poetry press Sidekick Books. Her poetry has been shortlisted for the Forward and Bridport Prizes, translated into Russian and Spanish and thrown out of a helicopter. She'd like to thank her own father for enriching her life with Louise Brooks bios, Classic Shell and Chris Farlowe's version of 'Out of Time'.

Max Maher, from Bexhill-on-Sea in East Sussex, is currently studying English at Cambridge University. He tries to creatively depict honest emotion in his poetry and his biggest inspirations are JD Salinger and singer-songwriter Conor Oberst.

Born in West Hartlepool, County Durham, **Martin Malone** now lives in Warwickshire. He won the 2011 Straid Poetry Award and the 2012 Mirehouse Prize, and his first full collection, *The Waiting Hillside*, is published by Templar Poetry. Currently studying for a PhD in poetry at Sheffield University, he edits *The Interpreter's House* poetry journal.

Harry Man was born in 1982. His poetry has appeared in *New Welsh Review, Poems in the Waiting Room* and elsewhere. He holds an MA in Creative Writing from Bath Spa University. His first pamphlet, *Lift* (tall-lighthouse, 2013), won the UNESCO Bridges of Struga Award.

Katrina Naomi is completing a creative writing PhD at Goldsmiths focusing on violence in poetry. Her work has appeared in *The TLS, Poetry Review* and *The Spectator*. Her collection *The Girl with the Cactus Handshake* (Templar Poetry, 2009) was shortlisted for the London New Poetry Award. Katrina was the first writer-in-residence at the Bronte Parsonage Museum. www.katrinanaomi.co.uk

Richard O'Brien's first pamphlet, *your own devices*, appeared in 2009 with tall-lighthouse press and his second, *The Emmores*, was published by The Emma Press in January 2014. His work has featured in *Poetry London*, the *Erotic Review, The Salt Book of Younger Poets* and *The Best British Poetry 2013*. His blog, *The Scallop-Shell*, is dedicated to the close reading of contemporary poetry.

Rachel Piercey is an editor at *The Cadaverine* magazine and The Emma Press. Her illustrated pamphlet of love poems, *The Flower and the Plough*, was published by The Emma Press in 2013 and a second pamphlet, *Rivers Wanted*, is forthcoming in October 2014.

Stevie Ronnie lives in rural Northumberland where he works as a writer and multi-disciplinary artist. His first full-length poetry collection is *Manifestations* (Red Squirrel Press, 2013). Stevie is currently working on a series of visual and literary works inspired by a recent residency in the High Arctic. http://stevieronnie.com

Jacqueline Saphra has won several awards including first prize in the Ledbury Poetry Competition. Her pamphlet, *Rock'n'Roll Mamma*, was published by Flarestack and her first full collection, *The Kitchen of Lovely Contraptions* (flipped eye, 2011) was developed with funding from Arts Council England and nominated for The Aldeburgh First Collection Prize. An illustrated book of prose poems is forthcoming from the Emma Press in 2014.

John Saunders' first collection, *After the Accident,* was published in 2010. His second full collection, *Chance,* was published in April 2013 by New Binary Press. His poems have been published in anthologies including *The Scaldy Detail 2013* and *The Poetry of Sex* (Penguin, 2014). John is a 2014 Pushcart Nominee.

Tom Sheehan served in Korea in 1951. His publications include: *Epic Cures; Brief Cases, Short Spans; Collection of Friends; From the Quickening; Korean Echoes; The Westering* (a National Book Award nomination); *Murder at the Forum; Death of a Lottery Foe; Death by Punishment;* and *An*

Accountable Death. He has 24 Pushcart nominations and his next collection of short stories, *In the Garden of Long Shadows*, is publishing in 2014.

Di Slaney was born in 1966 and lives on a Nottinghamshire smallholding with more animals than is sensible. She runs a marketing business and co-owns Candlestick Press. Di has been published in various magazines, including *Magma, The Rialto, The Interpreter's House, Brittle Star, LeftLion* and *Lighten Up Online.*

Jon Stone was born in Derby and is currently based in London. His collection, *School of Forgery*, was a Poetry Book Society recommendation and he won an Eric Gregory Award in 2012. He's also co-creator of Sidekick Books (www.drfulminare.com), publishers of collaborative creative anthologies.

Richard Thompson is a clinical psychologist. He grew up in rural Nova Scotia, Canada, and now lives and works in Texas. His poems have previously appeared in *Scissors and Spackle, Empirical Magazine* and *Skive Magazine*, among others.

Jerrold Yam is a law undergraduate at University College London and the author of *Intruder* (2014), *Scattered Vertebrae* (2013) and *Chasing Curtained Suns* (2012). His poems have been published in more than eighty literary journals and anthologies across twenty countries. He has received literary awards from the British Council, Poetry Book Society and National University of Singapore, and is the youngest Singaporean to be nominated for the Pushcart Prize.

THE EMMA PRESS

small press, big dreams

The Emma Press is an independent publisher dedicated to producing books which are sweet, funny and beautiful. It was founded in 2012 in Winnersh, UK, by Emma Wright and the first Emma Press book, *The Flower and the Plough* by Rachel Piercey, was published in January 2013.

Our current publishing programme includes a mixture of themed poetry anthologies and single-author pamphlets, with an ongoing engagement with the works of the Roman poet Ovid. We publish poems and books which excite us, and we are often on the lookout for new writing to feature in our latest projects.

Visit our website and sign up to the Emma Press newsletter to hear about all upcoming calls for submissions as well as our events and publications. You can also purchase our other titles and poetry-related stationery in our online shop.

http://theemmapress.com

Also from the Emma Press:

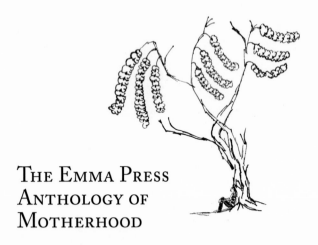

The Emma Press Anthology of Motherhood

ISBN: 978 0 9574596 7 0
Price: £10 / $17

Love and devotion sit alongside exhaustion and doubt in this profoundly moving collection of poems about mothers and the state of motherhood.

Edited by Rachel Piercey and Emma Wright, with poems from Deborah Alma, Stephanie Arsoska, Liz Berry, Sara Boyes, Carole Bromley, Laura Chalar, George David Clark, Flora de Falbe, Kate Garrett, Hilary Gilmore, Melinda Kallasmae, David Kennedy, Anna Kirk, Anna Kisby, Peter LaBerge, Eve Lacey, Anna Leader, Marena Lear, Katherine Lockton, Rachel Long, Julie Maclean, Ikhda Ayuning Maharsi, Kathryn Maris, Richard O'Brien, Rachel Piercey, Clare Pollard, Jacqueline Saphra, Kathryn Simmonds, Lavinia Singer, Catherine Smith, Camellia Stafford and Megan Watkins.

A Poetic Primer for Love and Seduction: Naso was my Tutor

ISBN: 978 0 9574596 3 2
Price: £10 / $17

Romantic adventurers! Look no further for your new handbook, your trusty adviser in matters of the heart, bedroom and boudoir. Forget the Game! Ditch the Rules! The Poetic Primer contains all you need to know about love, seduction, relationships and heartbreak. Inspired by Roman poet Ovid's *Ars Amatoria* (The Art of Lovemaking) and *Remedia Amoris* (The Cure for Love).

Edited by Rachel Piercey and Emma Wright, with poems from Jo Brandon, John Canfield, Jade Cuttle, Amy Key, Anja Konig, Cheryl Moskowitz, Abigail Parry, Rachel Piercey, Richard O'Brien, Christopher Reid, Jacqueline Saphra, Liane Strauss, Nicola Warwick, Ruth Wiggins and Andrew Wynn Owen.

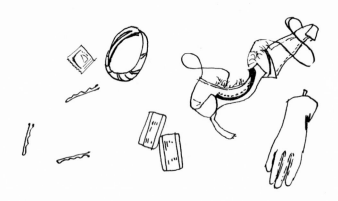

The Emma Press Anthology of
Mildly Erotic Verse

ISBN: 978 0 9574596 2 5
Price: £10 / $17

A beautiful anthology which celebrates modern eroticism
in all its messy, sexy glory. We see lovers imagined as
heroes and hares; describing what they want in jawdrop-
ping detail (or maybe with no words at all); meeting at
swimming pools, sinking into baths and magic boxes. They
wonder about lost knickers, worry about caravans, and –
sometimes – find themselves transformed.

Edited by Rachel Piercey and Emma Wright, with poems
from Julia Bird, Mel Denham, Joy Donnell, Hugh Dunkerley,
Kirsten Irving, Amy Key, Anja Konig, Ikhda Ayuning Ma-
harsi, Julie Mullen, Richard O'Brien, Emma Reay, Kristen
Roberts, Jacqueline Saphra, Lawrence Schimel, Stephen
Sexton, Jon Stone, Sara-Mae Tuson, Ruth Wiggins and
Jerrold Yam.

Captain Love
and the Five Joaquins

by John Clegg

ISBN: 978 1 910139 01 1
Price: £5 / $9
An Emma Press Pick

John Clegg (Society of Authors 2013 Eric Gregory Award)
thrills and intrigues with this true adventure story, set in
the vividly-evoked Old West and told through verse and
prose poems. The book follows the progress of bounty
hunter Captain Harry Love on his tour of California with
the supposed head of horse-thief Joaquin Murrieta in a jar.
The Five Joaquins, a notorious gang of outlaws, are hard on
Love's heels. As Love is lauded for his triumph over Murrieta,
his fear of exposure becomes unbearable.

The Held and the Lost

by Kristen Roberts

ISBN: 978 0 9574596 8 7
Price: £5 / $9
An Emma Press Pick

A moving collection of distinctly Australian poems about love, marriage and family life. Kristen Roberts is laid-back but precise as she sketches out sympathetic portraits of characters and relationships against the backdrop of swaying eucalypts, roses and occasional rain. These are love poems with their eyes wide open and scars defiantly on display.

The Emmores
by Richard O'Brien

ISBN: 978 0 9574596 4 9
Price: £5 / $9
An Emma Press Pick

Richard O'Brien (Foyle Young Poets of the Year Award winner, 2006 and 2007) deploys every trick in the love poet's book in this fascinating pamphlet of poems, written in response to a new long-distance relationship and loosely inspired by the Roman poet Ovid's *Amores*. An irresistible mix of tender odes, introspective sonnets, exuberant free verse and anthems of sexual persuasion.

The Flower and the Plough,
by Rachel Piercey

ISBN: 978 0 9574596 0 1
Price: £5 / $9
An Emma Press Pick

Rachel Piercey (Newdigate Prize, 2008) considers the dynamics of love and relationships in this stunning debut collection. Romantic but never sentimental, Piercey approaches her subject with emotional and linguistic clarity and builds up a nuanced study of passion and heartbreak, capturing everything from the extravagant surrender of early love to the raw ache and pain that can follow.

Raspberries for the Ferry
by Andrew Wynn Owen

ISBN: 978 0 9574596 5 6
Price: £6.50 / $12
An Emma Press Pamphlet

Andrew Wynn Owen dazzles in his debut pamphlet, embracing a variety of formal structures and whisking the reader up with his infectious rhythms and lively sensuality. Tortoises, dancers, lovers and whales all beguile in poems which are playful, charming and frequently heartfelt, grounded in the past and bubbling with modern verve. *Raspberries for the Ferry* is a veritable treasury of gorgeous, tart, juicy poems.

Ikhda, by Ikhda
by Ikhda Ayuning Maharsi

ISBN: 978 0 9574596 6 3
Price: £6.50 / $12
An Emma Press Pamphlet

Characters and landscapes leap off every page and the poems pulse with a visceral humanity as Maharsi glories in the possibilities of language and life. Reading this book is like being splashed with freezing water and showered with popping candy and wild roses – surprising, refreshing and bewildering, and something you won't forget in a hurry.

Coming soon:

THE DEAD SNAIL DIARIES, *by Jamie McGarry*

Publishing July 2014

A celebration of snail culture, as told by a talented and prematurely-crushed snail poet and translated by Jamie McGarry.

THE EMMA PRESS ANTHOLOGY OF HOMESICKNESS AND EXILE

Publishing September 2014

A collection of poems about home and belonging, as well as the idea of chosen homes, rootlessness, and emotional and physical exile.

OILS, *by Stephen Sexton*

Publishing October 2014

Belfast poet Stephen Sexton evokes melancholy and a strange kind of romance throughout his brilliant debut pamphlet.

RIVERS WANTED, *by Rachel Piercey*

Publishing October 2014

Rachel Piercey charms and disturbs in this beautiful, frequently heart-breaking collection of poems about love, identity and home.